Spies!

Real People, Real Stories

by Laura Portalupi

Reading Consultant:
Timothy Rasinski, Ph.D.
Professor of Reading Education
Kent State University

Content Consultant:
Gene Poteat
President, Association of
Former Intelligence Officers

Red Brick™ Learning

Published by Red Brick™ Learning
7825 Telegraph Road, Bloomington, Minnesota 55438
http://www.redbricklearning.com

Library of Congress Cataloging-in-Publication Data
Portalupi, Laura, 1981–
     Spies! real people, real stories / by Laura Portalupi.
     p. cm.—(High five reading)
     Summary: Discusses the history of spying from biblical times to the
present, types of spying, tools spies use, and the personal qualifications and
training of spies, and includes profiles of famous spies and a visit to the
International Spy Museum in Washington, D.C.
Includes bibliographical references and index.
     ISBN 0-7368-2788-9 (cloth)—ISBN 0-7368-2830-3 (pbk.)
     1. Spies—Juvenile literature. 2. Spies—Biography—Juvenile literature.
3. Espionage—Juvenile literature. [1. Spies. 2. Espionage.] I. Title. II. Series.
UB270.5.P67 2003
327.12—dc21
                              2003009764

Created by Kent Publishing Services, Inc.
Designed by Signature Design Group, Inc.
This publisher has made every effort to trace ownership of all copyrighted
material and to secure necessary permissions. In the event of any questions
arising as to the use of any material, the publisher, while expressing regret for
any inadvertent error, will be happy to make necessary corrections.

Photo Credits:
Cover, Rick Gayle/Corbis; page 4, courtesy of Samuel E. Poteat; page 9, Araldo
de Luca/Corbis; pages 7, 10, 18, 27, Bettmann/Corbis; page 11, AFP/Corbis;
pages 12 (left), 12 (right), 19, 25, The National Archives Image Library; page 14,
Dorling Kindersley Images; page 15, NewsCom; pages 16, 43, International Spy
Museum; page 20, Hulton Archive/Getty Images; page 28, Michael
Bryant/Philadelphia Inquirer; page 33, Blake Sell/Reuters Photo Archive; page
34, Digital Globe/Getty Images; page 36, USAF/Getty Images; page 39,
Kimimsa Mayama/Reuters Photo Archive; page 40, Cat Gwynn/Corbis

Printed in the United States of America.

1 2 3 4 5 6 08 07 06 05 04 03

Table of Contents

CHAPTER 1

History of Spies

Have you ever wanted to learn something secret? What did you do to learn the secret? Did you get caught? People have been trying to learn secrets and not get caught for a long time. For some, it's their job. These people are called spies.

FOR IDENTIFICATION ONLY

This is to certify that
Samuel E. POTRAT

whose photograph, signature and description appear hereon, is an employee of the United States Government

CENTRAL INTELLIGENCE AGENCY

No. 3145 1 July 62 *Francis M. Farrell*
EXPIRES: FOR THE DIRECTOR OF SECURITY

Identification card of a former CIA employee

Why Do Spies Spy?

There are many reasons people spy. During a war, a spy may try to figure out the enemy's plans. Secret information like this is called *intelligence*. Knowing these plans might help a country's leaders protect its people.

Another kind of spying is called *industrial espionage*. An industrial spy wants to know the secrets of another company. For example, a spy might try to learn how a product is made.

So, spies and spying are really nothing new. In fact, you might be surprised at where some of the first spy stories can be found.

---

information: facts about a person, place, thing, etc.
intelligence: secret information
industrial espionage: spying to learn the secrets of another business

The First Spies

Some of the oldest spy stories are found in the Old Testament. This is a holy book for Jews and Christians.

Around the 14th century B.C., the Israelites (IZ-ray-ah-lites) wanted to take land from the Canaanites (KAY-nah-nites). The Israelite leader, Moses, sent spies to find out how strong the Canaanites were.

The spies returned and told everyone that the Canaanites were very strong and would fight hard. But the Israelites did not like this message. They shouted to kill the spies!

Years later, Joshua was the leader of the Israelites. He had been one of Moses' first spies. Joshua sent two spies into a Canaanite city called Jericho. He wanted the spies to bring back clues that would help him destroy Jericho.

Israelite: a person who believed in one God and lived in what is now Israel
Canaanite: a person who believed in many gods and lived in what is now Israel

The spies hid in a woman's house. Her name was Rahab. But the king of Jericho learned of the spies anyway. He sent soldiers to Rahab's house. But Rahab lied to the soldiers and the spies got away.

The spies told Joshua what he wanted to know. Joshua's army attacked and destroyed Jericho. But they did not kill Rahab. Joshua protected Rahab and her family because she had helped his spies.

Rahab hid spies in her house.

Smart Spies

Alexander the Great (356–323 B.C.) was king of Macedon. But he wanted more. In fact, he wanted to conquer the world. His greatest enemies were the Persians. Alexander sent spies to find the best way to attack them.

The spies kept their information a secret. To do this, they wrote on a long, thin scroll that was wrapped around a stick. When the scroll was unrolled, the message was mixed up. The enemy could not read it.

But Alexander knew how to read the message. He just wrapped the scroll around a stick of the same size. Alexander never lost a single battle.

Alexander's spies used scrolls like this one to send secret messages.

---

conquer: to get by using force; to take over
scroll: a roll of paper with writing on it

Map of Alexander the Great's Empire at its largest, around 320 B.C.

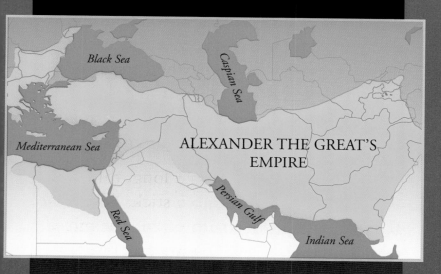

Black Sea

Caspian Sea

Mediterranean Sea

ALEXANDER THE GREAT'S EMPIRE

Red Sea

Persian Gulf

Indian Sea

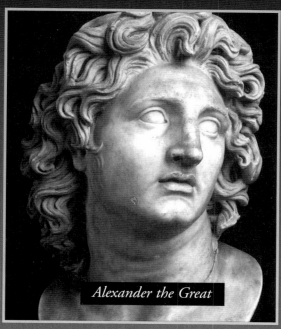

Alexander the Great

False Spies

Sun Tzu was a Chinese general in the fourth century B.C. Sun Tzu also used spies, but in a way that might surprise you. He tricked his own spies! Sun Tzu gave his spies false information and sent them into enemy land. Then he made sure they were caught. The enemy would then torture his spies until they told their information.

Of course, the information was false! Sun Tzu would then surprise his enemy with a different plan. What a cruel way to trick your enemy, by lying to your friends!

Sun Tzu wrote about spies in *The Art of War*. He wrote that spies would always be needed for an army to win a war.

Sun Tzu

torture: to cause someone great pain or mental suffering

Ghostly Spies

In the 12th century, Japanese princes used spies called *ninja*. These spies were also silent assassins. A prince would send a ninja to spy on and sometimes kill his enemy.

Ninja were rarely caught. They were in good shape so they could move quickly. They dressed in black to make it hard to see them at night. *Ninja* comes from Japanese words meaning "invisible person."

Spies have been around for centuries. Over the years, they have created many tools to help them spy. What tools do you think a spy might use?

A Ninja master poses in the city of Ueno, where ninjas first began. Ninjas worked as spies and silent assassins.

assassin: someone who kills a well-known or important person

11

Chapter 2

Tools and Tricks

What do spies do to get information? How do they share the information when they get it? And how do they keep from getting caught?

Makeup, a mustache, glasses, a hat, and different clothes give this man a new look.

In Disguise

Spies are said to be the masters of disguise. A spy usually tries to look and act like an everyday person. Sometimes a spy pretends to be someone else. A change of clothes, a new hairstyle, and a false name can hide who a spy really is.

A spy must also have a story that people believe. For example, Yvonne Cormeau (kor-MOH) was a British spy in France during World War II (1939–1945). She posed as a nurse named Annette. Her mission was to send secret German radio messages back to Britain.

Before leaving for France, Cormeau got new clothes. The clothes had to look French. Even the tags inside were removed. If someone saw that they were made in Britain, she would be caught.

---

disguise: a costume that hides who a person is
pose: to act; to pretend to be someone you are not

I Can Hear You!

Sometimes a spy wants to listen but not be seen. Maybe a secret meeting is going on and a spy wants to "listen in." What if the spy can't get close enough to hear?

Spies can use a "bug" to record people talking. A bug is a tiny microphone. It can be hidden in a wall, a desk, or even a pen. A bug has a transmitter. This transmitter sends out a radio signal.

Once a bug is planted, the spy finds the signal on a radio. Now the spy can listen to people talking near the bug. The spy may listen to a secret conversation more than 2,000 feet (800 meters) away!

This pen is really a listening tool. A mini microphone and transmitter are built into it.

---

microphone: a tool that picks up sound
transmitter: a tool that sends out sound

This wristwatch camera allowed a spy to take photographs while pretending to check his watch for the time of day.

Hidden Cameras

A spy may use a secret camera. Tiny cameras can be hidden in watches, neckties, purses, and even in food. When a spy uses one of these cameras, no one knows it is there!

A spy may use a microdot camera to take pictures of secret messages or files. These photos are called *microdots*. A microdot can be hidden on a piece of paper. It looks like the period at the end of this sentence. It is so small, no one notices it.

When the spy reaches safety, she can use an enlarger to read the message on the microdot.

---

microdot: a very small photo
enlarger: a tool that makes something look larger than it is

Secret Weapons

Spies do not usually carry weapons. During wartime they may do this, though. Weapons can be disguised as simple objects. A spy may carry a pencil with a small knife inside. Another kind of pencil works like a gun. Even a coin can hide a secret blade!

Called "The Kiss of Death," this lipstick gun was used by Soviet spies during the 1960s. It looked like a tube of lipstick. A spy could hide it in a purse or pocket.

Code Makers, Code Breakers

Sometimes a secret message is sent using "code." A code may use numbers, symbols, other letters, or even sounds instead of words. Only those who know the code can understand the message.

Navajo (NAV-uh-hoh) Indians helped send "coded" messages during World War II. Navajo is a complex language. For a long time the language was only spoken, not written. Only those who spoke Navajo could understand it.

Six Navajo code talkers helped U.S. forces during the battle of Iwo Jima in 1945. In two days, they sent and received more than 800 messages!

Sometimes an enemy will discover a coded message. Then enemy code-breakers try to figure out, or "break" the code. If it is a good code, the message will stay secret. The enemy never broke the Navajo code.

---

symbol: a mark that stands for something else
complex: not simple; hard to understand

Spying Computers

Some spies can do their work and not even leave home. A spy may use computer programs to break into private computer networks. This lets the spy read other people's files. He can steal secret information from thousands of miles away!

Spies often use complex tools to do their job. But they also use simple tricks. All of these tools and tricks are called *tradecraft.*

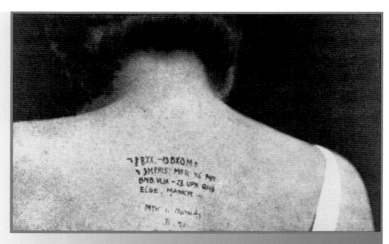

A Belgian spy carried messages written on her back in invisible ink.

---

network: a group of things that are connected

Funny Feet

During World War II, some British and American spies were trained in sabotage. They destroyed roads and bridges. This made it hard for enemy troops to get supplies they needed.

Some of these spies were sent to sabotage the Japanese in eastern Asia. When the spies secretly landed on a beach, they wore special shoes. The bottoms of the shoes looked like bare feet. So the spies' footprints made it look like local people had just been out for a walk on the beach!

This special shoe can make footprints in sand or dirt.

Spies work in secret. Still, some spies get caught. Others we learn about after their work is done. In the next chapter, you'll meet some famous spies.

---

sabotage: an act that hurts another person's work or other activity

CHAPTER 3

Famous Spies

Most famous spies are spies that were caught. Others were wartime spies who became famous after the war ended. Can you think of any famous spies? What do you know about them?

George Washington with Nathan Hale

The Young Patriot

During the Revolutionary War (1775–1783), General George Washington led rebel troops against the British. These colonists did not want to be ruled by Great Britain any longer.

Washington asked his troops for someone to spy on the British soldiers. At first, no one would do it. They believed spying was not for gentlemen. Then Nathan Hale agreed to spy. He was 21 years old and very patriotic.

Hale spied on British army camps. He drew maps to show where the camps were. He hid these maps in his shoes. But the British caught Hale and found the maps. They executed Hale for being a spy. He had only been on the job for one week!

---

colonist: a person who lived in one of the first 13 colonies forming the United States
patriotic: having great love for one's country
execute: to kill someone for breaking the law

Spies Who Should Be Famous

A spy may get more information if the enemy trusts her. During the Civil War (1861–1865), Mary Bowser had the trust of Confederate President Jefferson Davis. At the time, many people thought women and slaves were not smart or brave enough to spy.

Bowser, a former slave, was a servant in Davis's office. She often saw important papers on his desk. Sometimes she even saw his battle plans.

Bowser had a very good memory. She told her friend, Elizabeth Van Lew, what she had seen. Van Lew then gave this information to Union officers. Some of it helped the Union win the war.

Confederate: a person or state that no longer wanted to be part of the United States during the Civil War

Union: a person or state that supported the United States during the Civil War

When the war ended, General Ulysses S. Grant honored Van Lew for her work. The first Union flag in Richmond, Virginia, was raised at her house.

In 1995, Bowser was finally honored. Her name was added to the U.S. Army Intelligence Hall of Fame.

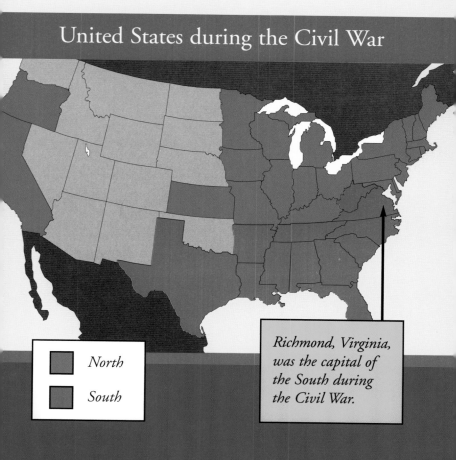

United States during the Civil War

North

South

Richmond, Virginia, was the capital of the South during the Civil War.

Tricked, but Not Defeated

In 1940, Odette Sansom was a mother raising three young daughters. She was born in France but lived in England. When the Germans took over France at the start of World War II, she took action.

Sansom started working for the Special Operations Executive (SOE) in England. The SOE sent people to help the French Resistance. This was a secret group in France. They used spies and sabotage to try to stop the Germans.

Sansom went to France and worked with the Resistance. She spied there for many months.

Then, a German spy tricked a member of the Resistance. The spy lied and said that he wanted to join the group. When he joined, he got the names of SOE spies.

French Resistance: a secret group trying to stop the Germans from taking over France

Sansom was caught and tortured. They beat her and pulled out all of her toenails. But she never told the Germans anything about her work.

In 1945, Sansom was freed by the Allies. She was very sick, but she survived. For a year, she could not wear shoes because of the torture.

In 1950, the United Kingdom awarded Sansom the George Cross. She was the first woman to win this award. The George Cross is the United Kingdom's highest award for bravery.

Odette Sansom

The Spy Who Played Baseball

Moe Berg played major-league baseball for 16 years. But that's not all he did. When he stopped playing baseball in 1939, he spied for the United States during World War II.

Berg spoke nine languages! He liked to learn about foreign countries. He liked to travel. He was good at fitting in wherever he went.

In 1944, Berg posed as a college student in Switzerland. He was 42 years old. He went to class to listen to a German scientist. The United States wanted Berg to find out if the Germans could build an atomic bomb. He reported back that they were not close to building a bomb.

After the war, Berg led a quiet life. He never lived in one place too long. Even Berg's friends wondered what secrets he might still have been hiding.

---

foreign: from another country
atomic bomb: a powerful bomb that explodes with great force, heat, and bright light

Moe Berg poses in his baseball uniform.

The famous spies in this chapter come from very different backgrounds. They include a servant, a young mother, and a baseball player. Did they have anything in common? Think about it.

— CHAPTER **4** —

Becoming a Spy

Being a spy is more than stealing an enemy's secrets. It's more than putting on a disguise. What do you think it takes to be a real spy?

Do You Have What It Takes?

Spies have some things in common. A good spy can think fast. If the enemy is closing in, a spy may have only seconds to change plans or get away.

Spying can be a dangerous job. Most spies are brave. They may face jail, torture, or even death if they are caught. Some spies get a thrill from the danger.

Many spies work for their government. These spies must be patriotic. They often collect information that governments use to protect their people. Some governments also use spies to steal secrets from other countries.

---

dangerous: likely to cause pain; unsafe

Education

Most U.S. government spies today have a college degree. They learn research and analytical skills at college. These skills help spies find and understand the information they seek. Sometimes a spy is an expert in one area, like computers or science.

Join the Club

Most spies in the world today do not work alone. They work for a country's government. In the United States, there are two main spy services.

The Federal Bureau of Investigation (FBI) tries to catch spies and people who commit crimes within the United States. The Central Intelligence Agency (CIA) sends U.S. spies to other countries. A person must be a U.S. citizen to spy for either the FBI or CIA.

---

research: studying to learn new facts or solve a problem
analytical: studying the parts of something
federal: run by a country

Famous Spy Services

FBI

The Federal Bureau of Investigation was formed in 1908 to protect citizens of the United States. The FBI also finds and catches foreign spies within the United States. Today, the FBI has more than 11,400 Special Agents.

CIA

The Central Intelligence Agency was created in 1947. The CIA sends spies to other countries to gather information. The CIA cannot spy on U.S. citizens.

KGB

The Committee of State Security was created in 1954 to protect the Soviet Union. In 1991, the Soviet Union broke into states. Russia took most of the KGB's powers.

Mossad

The Institute for Intelligence and Special Operations was formed in 1949 in Israel. Mossad sends spies to other countries to gather information.

MI5 and MI6

MI5 is the British Security Service. It was formed in 1909 to protect British citizens. MI5 catches spies in Britain. MI6 is the British Secret Intelligence Service. It was created in 1909 and sends British spies to other countries.

Getting the Job

To work for the FBI or CIA you must go through a careful background check. You may also need to take a lie detector test. The FBI and CIA want people they can trust. The FBI and CIA may also recruit people they think would be good spies.

Training

Today the FBI and CIA don't reveal much about their training. But most of it comes from spy training used in the 1940s. At that time, new spies had two types of training.

Basic training included survival, sabotage, and fighting skills. Advanced training taught spies different skills for different jobs. For example, a spy often learned another language if he or she was going to be sent to another country.

---

lie detector: a tool that can tell if someone is telling the truth
recruit: to ask a person to join
survival: staying alive

U.S. Secret Service agents practice their response to an attack on the president's car during a training exercise.

It's not easy to become a spy. The world of spying is always changing. What do you think some spy tools and missions of today might be?

mission: a job or task

— CHAPTER **5** —

Spying Today

Look up at the bright stars in the night sky. Some of those "stars" might not be stars at all. You might be looking at a spy tool!

The United States took satellite images like this one during the war with Iraq in 2003.

Technical Spying

Technical spying is a way to collect information using technology. Satellites are the most common tool for technical spying. These machines circle Earth from hundreds of miles away.

Satellites may take pictures of things on Earth. They can send these pictures back to Earth right away.

The United States used satellites during the war with Iraq in 2003. The satellites showed where Iraqi tanks and troops were. They also showed the damage caused by bombs. These pictures helped U.S. and other troops to plan what to do next.

Some satellites can take clear pictures of objects that are only 6 inches (15 centimeters) wide! Other satellites take clear images even when it is nighttime or cloudy.

---

technical: having to do with science
technology: the use of science and engineering to improve work and how people live
satellite: an object that is put into orbit around a planet or moon

A U.S. U-2 spy plane flies a United Nations inspection mission over Iraq.

Tools against Terrorism

Today, many governments use technical spying to protect their people from terrorism. Terrorists want to cause fear in people. Sometimes they do this by killing innocent people.

In 2001, almost 3,000 people were killed in a terrorist attack in the United States. After the attack, the FBI started using more aircraft for spying.

The FBI uses planes and helicopters to spy on people they think may be terrorists. They fly above places where terrorists may be hiding, training, or where they may strike. The aircraft have special tools. Some have cameras to follow people in the dark. Some have special receivers to listen to cell phone calls.

Most of the FBI's aircraft are disguised. They look just like planes or helicopters that anyone could fly in.

---

terrorism: the use of force to scare people
innocent: doing no harm; not guilty

New Missions

Today, some spies work to stop other kinds of violence and illegal sales. A spy may join a gang to learn where it gets its weapons. Often the weapons are illegal. This information helps the government catch those who sell and buy weapons. It also helps them catch people who use the weapons to commit crimes.

Technical spying is also used to stop illegal drug traffic. For example, a satellite can be used to spot fields where plants used to make drugs are being grown. A satellite can also spot airplane runways. People who make, buy, or sell drugs may use planes. The satellite takes pictures of the runways where they land and take off.

These pictures can then help the government catch people involved in such drug traffic.

---

violence: force used to harm
illegal: against the law
traffic: selling and buying goods against the law

A H-2A rocket carrying Japan's first spy satellites blasts off at Tanegashima Space Center on March 28, 2003.

The Internet

Spies also can use the Internet to gather and send information. For example, a spy may create a website. The spy may write a coded message to another spy and display it on this website. Most people won't notice the coded message. Only spies who know the code will be able to read it.

Spies may use the Internet to collect and send information.

Internet: a network of information linked by computers

Digital Steganography

Steganography is the practice of hiding messages. For example, a spy may have a picture that she needs to give to another spy. The spy can use a computer to make the picture very small. Then, she can hide the picture inside a larger picture. The secret picture is so tiny that it is impossible to see. Later on, another spy can enlarge the hidden picture, also using a computer.

The Secret World of Spying

Spying is one of the oldest jobs around. The way people spy is always changing, though. Today spies use more tools than ever before.

Spying is also a dangerous job. Yet some people love the thrill of spying. What about you? What do you think of the secret world of spying?

---

digital steganography: hiding messages with the use of electronics, such as a computer

Epilogue

International Spy Museum

Imagine being surrounded by more than 600 spy artifacts! The International Spy Museum has the world's largest public collection of spy artifacts.

The museum was built in 2002 in Washington, D.C. The exhibits there tell about famous spies, spy training, and spying today. Many displays are hands-on. You can even test your own spying skills.

The museum shows how technology has changed spying throughout the years. Still, maybe you will agree with the CIA agent who said that "the most powerful tool" hasn't changed at all. What tool is that? The human brain.

---

artifact: an object made by humans
exhibit: something shown to the public
hands-on: able to be touched or used

The International Spy Museum in Washington, D.C.

Glossary

analytical: studying the parts of something

artifact: an object made by humans

assassin: someone who kills a well-known or important person

atomic bomb: a powerful bomb that explodes with great force, heat, and bright light

Canaanite: a person who believed in many gods and lived in what is now Israel

colonist: a person who lived in one of the first 13 colonies forming the United States

complex: not simple; hard to understand

Confederate: a person or state that no longer wanted to be part of the United States during the Civil War

conquer: to get by using force; to take over

dangerous: likely to cause pain; unsafe

digital steganography: hiding messages with the use of electronics, such as a computer

disguise: a costume that hides who a person is

enlarger: a tool that makes something look larger than it is

execute: to kill someone for breaking the law

exhibit: something shown to the public

federal: run by a country

foreign: from another country

French Resistance: a secret group trying to stop the Germans from taking over France

hands-on: able to be touched or used

illegal: against the law

industrial espionage: spying to learn the secrets of another business

information: facts about a person, place, thing, etc.

innocent: doing no harm; not guilty

intelligence: secret information

Internet: a network of information linked by computers

Israelite: a person who believed in one God and lived in what is now Israel

lie detector: a tool that can tell if someone is telling the truth

microdot: a very small photo

microphone: a tool that picks up sound

mission: a job or task

network: a group of things that are connected

patriotic: having great love for one's country

pose: to act; to pretend to be someone you are not

recruit: to ask a person to join

research: studying to learn new facts or solve a problem

sabotage: an act that hurts another person's work or other activity

satellite: an object that is put into orbit around a planet or moon

scroll: a roll of paper with writing on it

survival: staying alive

symbol: a mark that stands for something else

technical: having to do with science

technology: the use of science and engineering to improve work and how people live

terrorism: the use of force to scare people

torture: to cause someone great pain or mental suffering

traffic: selling and buying goods against the law

transmitter: a tool that sends out sound

Union: a person or state that supported the United States during the Civil War

violence: force used to harm

Bibliography

Farman, John. *The Short and Bloody History of Spies*. Short and Bloody Histories. Minneapolis: Lerner Publications, 2002.

Manley, Claudia B. *Secret Agents: Life as a Professional Spy*. Extreme Careers. New York: Rosen Publishing, 2001.

Platt, Richard. *Spies!* DK Readers. New York: Dorling Kindersley, 2000.

Platt, Richard. *Spy*. Eyewitness Books. New York: Alfred A. Knopf, 1996.

Yancey, Diane. *Spies*. History Makers. San Diego: Lucent Books, 2002.

Ziff, John. *Espionage and Treason*. Crime, Justice, and Punishment. Philadelphia: Chelsea House, 2000.

Useful Addresses

Association of Former Intelligence Officers
6723 Whittier Avenue, Suite 303A
McLean, Virginia 22101-4533

International Spy Museum
800 F Street NW
Washington, D.C. 20004

Internet Sites

Association of Former Intelligence Officers
http://www.afio.com

CIA's Homepage for Kids
http://www.cia.gov/cia/ciakids/index.shtml

FBI Youth Grades 6th–12th
http://www.fbi.gov/kids/6th12th/6th12th.htm

International Spy Museum
http://www.spymuseum.org

Index